HOW TO DRAW AND COLOUR

STEAMPUNK

CHARACTERS

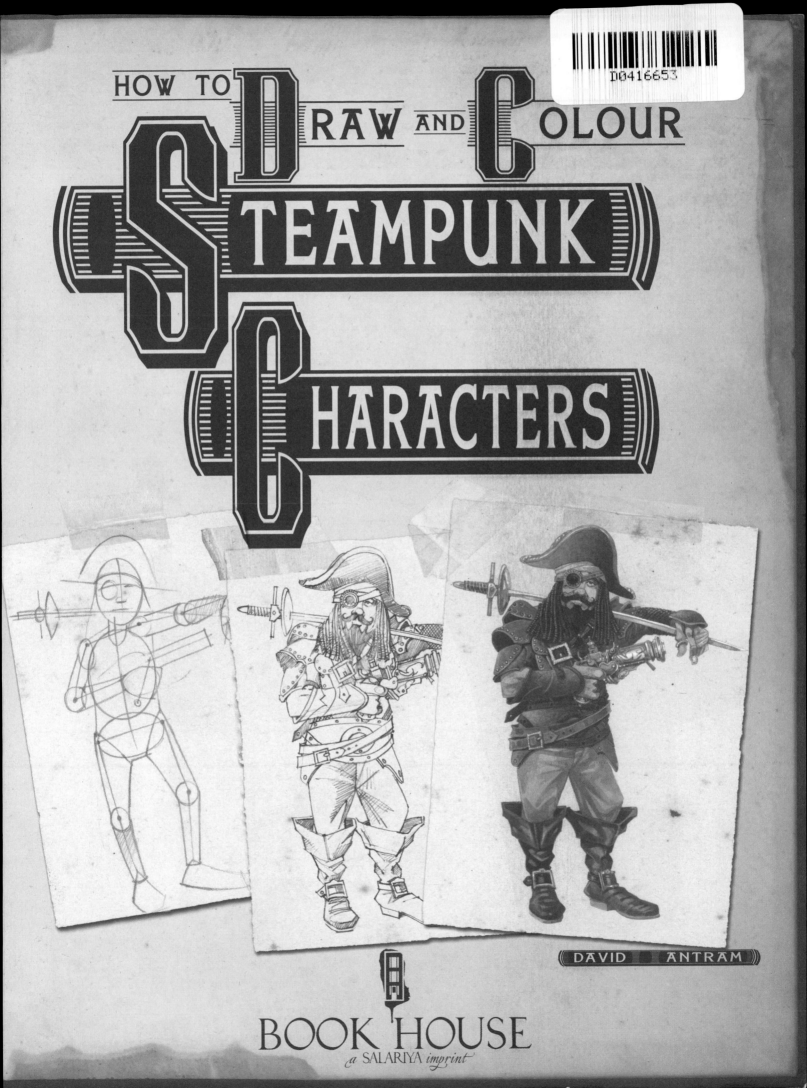

DAVID ANTRAM

BOOK HOUSE
a SALARIYA *imprint*

Published in Great Britain in MMXIV by
Book House, an imprint of
The Salariya Book Company Ltd
25 Marlborough Place, Brighton BN1 1UB
www.salariya.com
www.book-house.co.uk

PB ISBN-13: 978-1-908973-72-6

Editor: Stephen Haynes

1 3 5 7 9 8 6 4 2

A CIP catalogue record for this book is available
from the British Library.

Printed and bound in China.

Visit
www.salariya.com
for our online catalogue and
free interactive web books.

PAPER FROM
SUSTAINABLE
FORESTS

Contents

INTRODUCTION

Welcome to Steampunk – an artform that explores what the world might have been like if history had taken a slightly different turn. Taking its inspiration from a 19th-century view of the future, Steampunk shows us a world of high technology, but powered by steam and clockwork. It takes the fantastic ideas of writers such as Jules Verne and H. G. Wells, and updates them for the modern age. Futuristic equipment made of cast iron and brass, mahogany and leather, has a character that today's plastics and electronics can never achieve.

This book introduces you to some of the ingenious gentlemen and indomitable ladies who inhabit the world of Steampunk. Before you draw a character, take a moment to consider what kind of person they are and what kind of story they have to tell…

Aviatrix

Big-Game Hunter

4

Gentleman Inventor

Winged Girl

Sky Pirate

DRAWING TOOLS

You don't need a vast range of equipment for your Steampunk drawings – the pencil is your most versatile tool. But experiment with different ways of making marks, and find out what suits you. Here are some possibilities worth exploring.

Sky Pirate

Ink pens are ideal for sketching. Use layers of shading to develop different tones.

Inventor

Tone

Using tone (shading) makes your drawings look more realistic and three-dimensional. The darkest areas can be inked in solidly, leaving the lightest parts ink-free. Use hatching for midtones and cross-hatching for darker tones.

Cross-hatching   Hatching

Felt-tips are great for filling in areas of flat tone.

Dramatic use of light and dark tones is called chiaroscuro – an Italian word for 'light–dark'.

Aviatrix

Pencils

Pencils come in different grades, ranging from fine greys to soft, deep blacks.

Hard pencils are usually graded from H to 6H (the hardest). Soft pencils are graded from B to 9B (the softest and blackest).

HB pencils are between H and B. They are ideal for general sketching, but experiment with different grades of pencils and explore the range of tones they can produce.

Draughtsmen's pens

Draughtsmen's pens and art pens are ideal for creating fine, regular lines and surface texture, as in the Inventor portrait opposite. Pen nibs are available in a variety of widths.

Paper surfaces

Paper textures range from smooth to very rough. Rough paper is ideal for use with charcoal, whereas smooth paper is best for fine line drawings.

Scientist

The Scientist portrait is constructed from washes of ink diluted to different shades.

7

DEAS

Steampunk uses a mix of styles rooted in an alternative 19th century, when the British Empire vied with other colonial powers to rule the world with its coal-powered technology. Look for inspiration in old artefacts and vintage photographs such as these.

Fashion
Old fashions can give you a starting point for Steampunk outfits.

Army uniforms
Old army uniforms are a great source of inspiration. Pith helmets and leather belts are among the staples of Steampunk costume.

Science equipment
Scientific apparatus and gadgets from the gaslit past can make great accessories for your characters. Combine objects to invent your own mysterious accoutrements.

Hats

A hat can give a character a distinct personality. In Victorian times, a gentleman was not properly dressed without a top hat.

Welding

Welding goggles and equipment make good accessories for mechanically minded characters.

Aviation outfits

Aviators' clothes from the early 20th century are ideal for depicting the Steampunk legends of the skies.

Keep your eyes open!

Get inspiration from old costumes, photos and inventions found in museums. Interesting details are all around you.

POSES

Drawing stick figures helps to give you an understanding of the movement and proportions of your characters. It allows you to identify the most essential features of a pose.

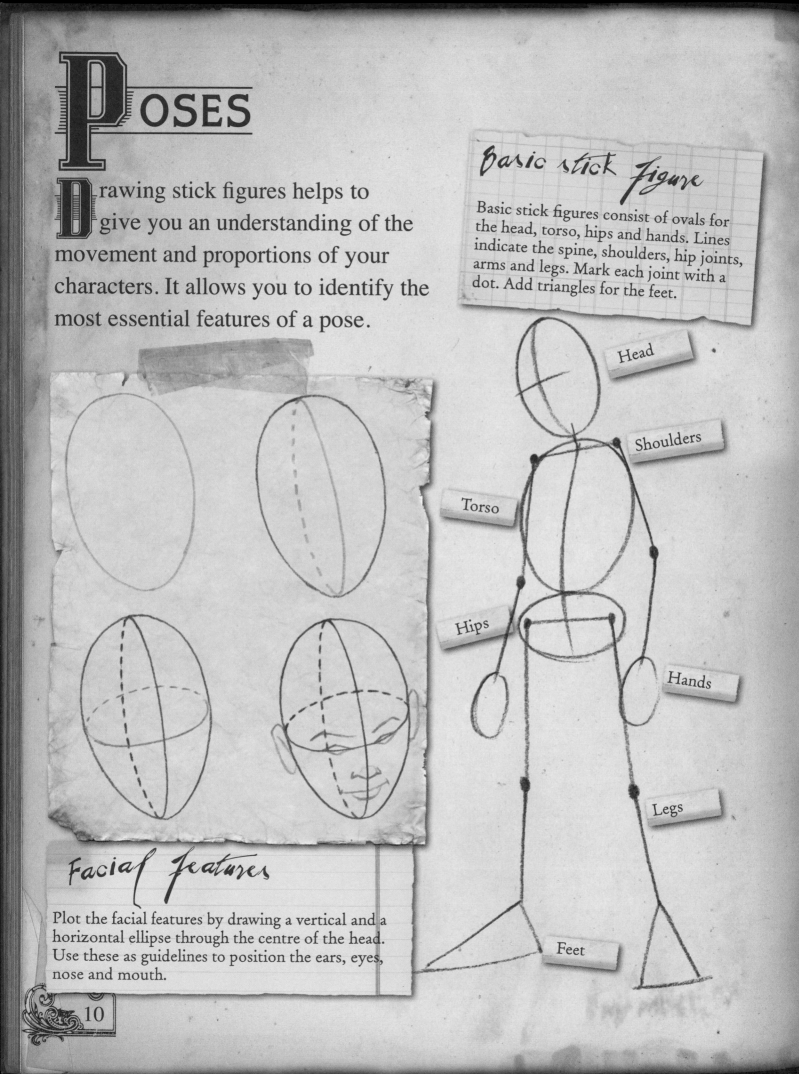

Head

Shoulders

Torso

Hips

Hands

Legs

Feet

Facial features

Plot the facial features by drawing a vertical and a horizontal ellipse through the centre of the head. Use these as guidelines to position the ears, eyes, nose and mouth.

Practise many different poses, including awkward and unusual ones. This will help you understand how the body moves.

STEAMPUNK ROBOTS

These robots look human on the surface, but beneath the skin they are whirring mechanical automata. Their remarkable abilities can be used for good or evil – which side will yours be on?

Sketch out a range of ideas before choosing the features that are worth developing.

Base your drawing on human anatomy but replace muscles, bones and skin with mechanical parts.

Pistons are ideal for bones, cogs make good joints and metal plating with rivets can look great as skin.

Try drawing the human face of your robot alongside a cutaway showing what lies beneath the skin.

Mechanical Lady

Automatic Gentleman

This automaton's stovepipe hat really lives up to its name: it has funnels to release steam.

Intricate gears and machinery operate flawlessy behind the human-looking face.

The mechanical jaw has razor-sharp teeth capable of immense biting pressure.

Superior robots like this model can easily be mistaken for real people.

Pistons and rods make up the collarbone.

Why not create a Steampunk cyborg? These are humans fitted with mechanical parts to enhance their powers.

SKY PIRATE

Dress your pirate in a mix of clothes from different periods, which he has plundered on his travels. Where has he been, and where might he go next?

Establish the pose by drawing a stick figure as on pages 10–11.

1

Add tube shapes and joints.

2

3

Start drawing in clothing and weapons.

4

Clean up the pencil drawing and add detail. Pencil in areas of light and shade.

14

5

Transferring

Transfer a light pencil outline onto paper or card, or use a light-box to trace your finished drawing.

6 Watercolour

This character has been painted in watercolours. The white of the paper forms the highlights. Thin washes of colour are then applied to the stretched paper. Further washes build up areas of colour.

Lighter areas have fewer washes. It is important not to labour watercolour painting, or the colour will lose its freshness. It's often better to work with a limited palette of colours.

Highlights

Add highlights using thin layers of white watercolour or gouache if necessary.

Paint one layer of flat colour.

Add washes to give shape.

INVENTOR

Professor Wheatstone creates ingenious optical devices by cannibalising any machinery to hand, whether clockwork or steam-powered.

1

Establish your inventor's pose by sketching in simple ovals and lines.

2

The professor's goggles are based on the contraption that opticians use for sight tests.

3

Gadgets

Get ideas for gadgets by looking at Victorian steam-driven machinery or devices such as early cameras.

16

4 Transferring

Transfer a light pencil outline onto paper or card, or use a light-box to trace your drawing.

5 Inking

Ink in the pencil lines and use a putty rubber (kneadable eraser) to remove any traces of pencil.

Use hatching and cross-hatching for shading, and solid black for the darkest areas.

BIG-GAME HUNTER

This fearsome individual stalks the jungles of far-flung continents looking for the most spectacular animals to boost his bizarre taxidermy collection. His eight-barrelled steam-powered shotgun can bring down the largest prey.

1

Sketch in the basic shapes using ovals for the head, body, hips and hands.

2

Add tube shapes to the figure, and a pith helmet and shotgun.

3

Lightly add detail to the character. Draw in the structure of the gun and add the ammunition belts.

4

Final pencil stages

Add more details to the gun, outfit and facial features.

Decide where the light is coming from in your drawing, and add shade to the parts that face away from the light. Create highlights with an eraser if necessary.

Rub out any unwanted construction lines.

5 ## Ink and watercolour

Ink in the pencil outlines using a fine ink pen.

Establish the basic colours of your character by painting in light colour washes.

Add a second wash of darker tones, creating shadows and folds.

Finally, strengthen the shadows and use a fine-pointed brush to define small details.

WINGED GIRL

Who is the Winged Girl, and what secret technology allows her to soar through the skies, landing at will in even the most heavily fortified locations?

Sketch a crouching stick figure. Add the position of the wings.

Add tube shapes to the figure, and a hat. Draw in the individual blades of the wings.

Draw in the fine details of the figure. Add shadows and highlights.

4

Add shading to the far wing to create a silhouette.

Use soft shading for light areas.

Pencil shading can produce a dramatic effect. A sharp pencil also creates precise lines that are ideal for a mechanical look.

Decide on your highlighted areas before you add colour, as coloured pencil is difficult to erase.

Coloured pencils

The intensity of the colour is determined by the pressure on the pencil.

Layering pencil colours can create new shades and build up interesting tones.

CIENTIST

At work in the ruins of his lab after an explosive experiment, the Scientist is convinced of his genius. He will stop at nothing to prove his supremacy to the world.

Draw a stick figure with ovals for the head, hand, body and hips.

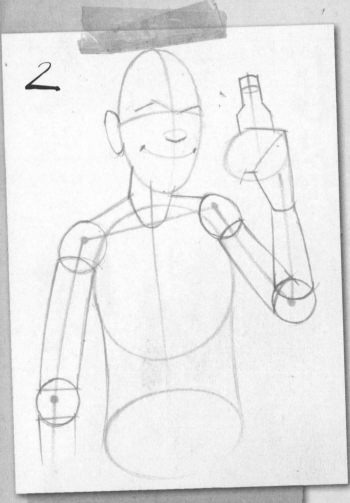

Add tube shapes to the stick figure. Position the facial features and add a laboratory bottle.

Draw in the scientist's outfit. Include welding goggles and a heavy-duty apron. Decide what his expression should be: kindly or menacing?

4

Add the final intricate details using a pencil.

5 Finishing in ink

Alternatively, complete the drawing by adding ink washes to build up tone.

Ink washes

Water-based ink washes change in tone depending on the amount of water added. The more water, the lighter the wash. Leave highlighted areas white.

A VIATRIX

This fearless heroine is the greatest pilot of the steam-powered skies. She can fly any airborne contraption with more skill than anyone else – man or woman.

Draw a seated figure with ovals for the head, torso, hips and hands. Add basic shapes for the feet.

Add tube shapes to the stick figure. Position the facial features and add the flight cap and hair contours.

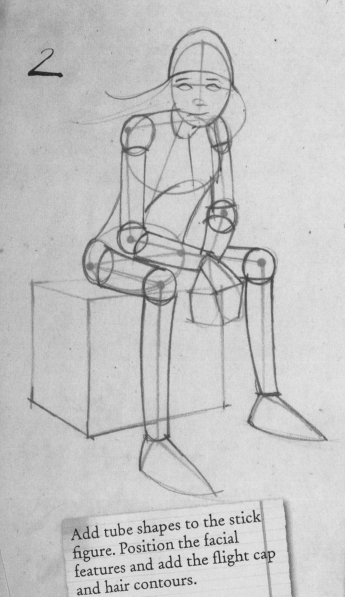

Sketch in clothes, boots and flying goggles. Add more detail to the face and hair.

4

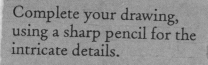

Complete your drawing, using a sharp pencil for the intricate details.

pencil tone

Varying the pressure of your pencil varies the tone. Combinations of light and dark tones can help to capture folds in fabric.

Highlights

Highlights such as the shine on the boots can be left white, or added by using an eraser.

Decide on your light source and add the darkest areas of tone in the parts that face away from the light.

GENTLEMAN INVENTOR

This dapper gent invents wondrous gadgets for the upper classes. He is sporting a fantastic invention: a steam-powered electric generator.

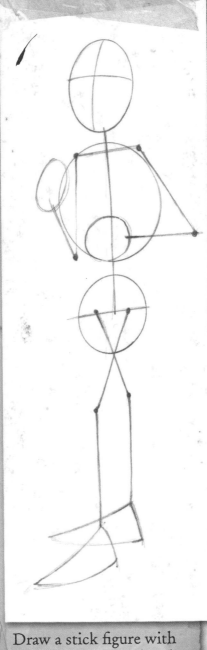

Draw a stick figure with ovals for the head, hands, body and hips.

Add tube shapes to the stick figure. Draw in the clothes, a top hat and the shape of the generator.

Add more detail to the clothing and sketch in the details of the generator.

4 *Colour stages*

5

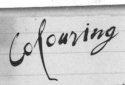

Colouring

Remove any unwanted construction lines and sharpen up your drawing. Now begin to add colour. Add basic flat colours first, then gradually build up the features with further layers, as shown above.

You can sharpen your image after colouring it by using a fine black pen to go over some of the lines.

Remember to leave the white of the paper for highlights.

COMIC STRIP 1

Making your own comic strip is a great way to bring your character ideas to life. This example shows a Steampunk aviatrix as she discovers a mechanical man and works out how to activate him to reveal his hidden secrets.

1 Planning

Work out your story first, then decide how many pictures you need to show it dramatically.

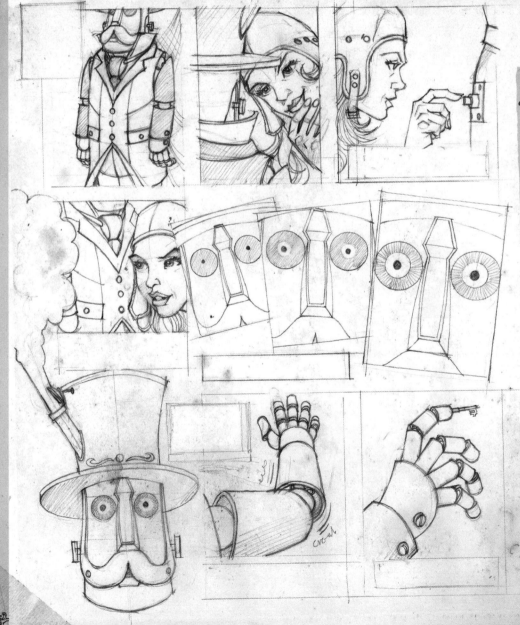

2 Sketching

Sketch your story frame by frame. This is called a storyboard. Include some close-ups to enhance the drama.

Leave some blank boxes for captions. These can help to explain the action or set the scene.

Don't worry about minor mistakes in the drawing; these can be corrected later. Concentrate on the composition, layout and storytelling.

Decide on the direction of the light source and keep this consistent throughout the comic-strip drawings.

Texture

Add detail to the characters. Give fabrics a sense of texture to contrast with the shiny mechanical parts.

Add a shot of steam and movement lines to the robot's arm to show it is powering up.

Storytelling

It is important for each image to express the story dynamically. For example, the lines radiating out from the hand (above) create a sense of tension.

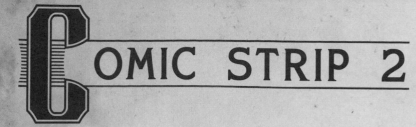

Here are two alternative finishes for your comic strip: ink outline, or full colour. If you want to colour it there are plenty of options, such as watercolour, coloured inks or acrylics. Be careful – mistakes at this stage aren't easy to fix.

Outlines

Instead of adding shade and tone to your comic strip, carefully ink over your finished lines with a pen. In this style, no shading is used.

Cleaning

When the ink is dry, remove any unwanted pencil lines with a soft rubber (eraser).

Colouring

Characters and backgrounds need to be coloured consistently so that readers can recognise them from one scene to the next.

Apply colour to your characters using a build-up of washes. Mix your colours so the washes can be added to each scene at the same time.

Either leave highlights white, or add them in white paint.

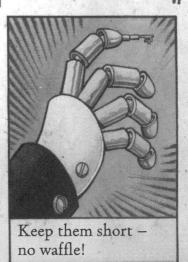

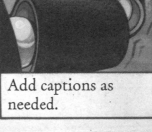

Add captions as needed.

Keep them short — no waffle!

Water-soluble pencils

These offer a versatile combination of drawing and painting. You can create colour washes by adding water.

Coloured pencils

Well-sharpened coloured pencils are also ideal for adding crisp lines to your drawing.

LOSSARY

Chiaroscuro — The use of light and dark in a drawing.

Cross-hatching — A series of criss–crossing lines used to add dark shading to a drawing.

Gouache — Opaque watercolour.

Hatching — A series of parallel lines used to add medium shading to a drawing.

Silhouette — A drawing that shows only a flat, dark shape, like a shadow.

Three–dimensional — Having an effect of depth, so as to look lifelike or real.

Wash — A transparent layer of colour, especially watercolour.

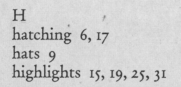NDEX